Mathematics

Book 4

- *Fractions*
- *Word problems*
- *Prime numbers*
- *Expanded forms*
- *Divison*
- *Multiples*
- *Factors*
- *Area*
- *Capacity*
- *Perimeter*
- *Measurement*

Purnima Sharma, M.A., B.Ed.

Number Extension

Read carefully and understand these numbers and their place value with the help of the given PLACE VALUE CHART.

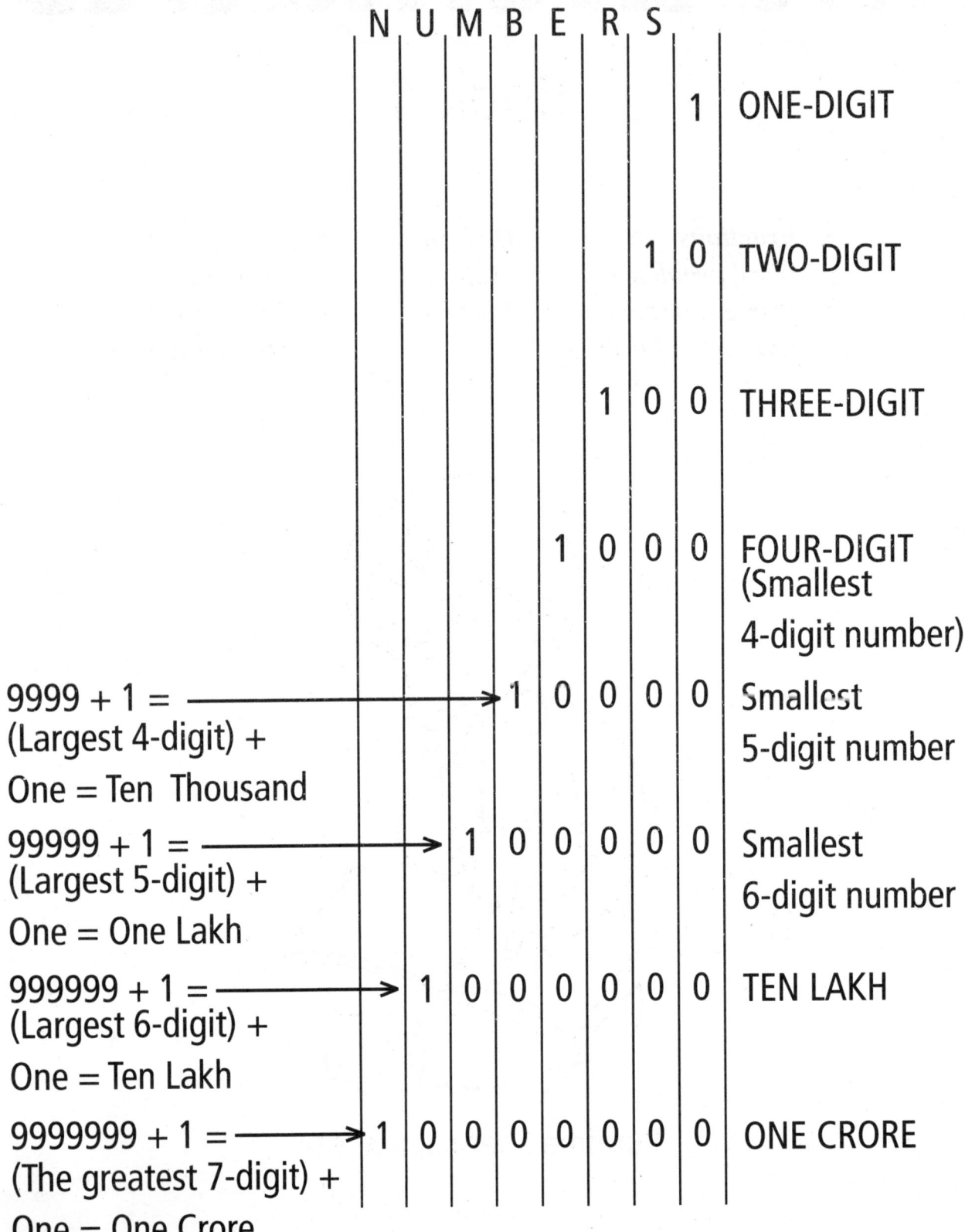

	N	U	M	B	E	R	S	
							1	ONE-DIGIT
						1	0	TWO-DIGIT
					1	0	0	THREE-DIGIT
				1	0	0	0	FOUR-DIGIT (Smallest 4-digit number)
9999 + 1 = (Largest 4-digit) + One = Ten Thousand				1	0	0	0	0	Smallest 5-digit number
99999 + 1 = (Largest 5-digit) + One = One Lakh			1	0	0	0	0	0	Smallest 6-digit number
999999 + 1 = (Largest 6-digit) + One = Ten Lakh		1	0	0	0	0	0	0	TEN LAKH
9999999 + 1 = (The greatest 7-digit) + One = One Crore	1	0	0	0	0	0	0	0	ONE CRORE

Now see the example done for you.
Add the smallest 5-digit number and the smallest 4-digit number.
Write in words too.

$$
\begin{array}{r}
10,000 \\
+1,000 \\
\hline
11,000
\end{array}
$$

= Eleven thousand

Do it yourself:-

1. Add the smallest 6-digit number and the smallest 5-digit number.

$$
\begin{array}{r}
1,00,000 \\
+10,000 \\
\hline

\end{array}
$$

Answer: _____

2. Subtract the smallest 3-digit number from the largest 4-digit number.

```
TH H T O
 9 9 9 9
-    1 0 0
_____
```

Answer: _____

3. Subtract the largest 4-digit number from the smallest 5-digit number.

```
TTh TH H T O
 1  0 0 0 0
-   9 9 9 9
_____
```

Answer: _____

4. Subtract the largest 3-digit number from largest 4-digit number.

```
TH H T O
 9 9 9 9
-  9 9 9
_____
```

Answer: _____

5. Write the place value of the underlined numbers.

   a. 1632 → = _____

   b. 777 → = _____

   c. 846 → = _____

   d. 179 → = _____

6. Write in words:-

   a. 4,000 → = Four thousand

   b. 748 → = _____

   c. 900 → = _____

   d. 804 → = _____

7. Write in figures:-

   a. Six hundred and ninety _____

   b. One thousand and seven hundred _____

   c. Five hundred and forty _____

   d. One thousand _____

8. Write in expanded form:-

   Example: 4763

   (4000 + 700 + 60 + 3)

   a. 8879 = _____

   b. 7845 = _____

   c. 6564 = _____

   d. 1500 = _____

9. Using the given digits form the greatest and the smallest numbers.

		Greatest	Smallest
a.	3,6,9	963	369
b.	4,7,2	742	247
c.	3,8,2	____	____
d.	6,1,9	____	____
e.	1,9,7	____	____
f.	5,0,6	____	____

Expanded Form and Standard Form

Writing a number in its **expanded form** means showing the place value of each digit in it. It can be done in 3 ways.

- $70{,}000 + 8{,}000 + 400 + 50 + 6 = 78{,}456$

- $7 \times 10{,}000 + 8 \times 1000 + 4 \times 100 + 5 \times 10 + 6 \times 1 = 78{,}456$

- 7 ten thousand + 8 thousand + 4 hundreds + 5 tens + 6 ones = 78,456

1. Write the given numbers in their expanded form. Follow the pattern above.

   a. Write the number 96,847 in its expanded form.

   - ....
   - ....
   - ....

   b. Write the number 85,978 in its expanded form.

   - ....
   - ....
   - ....

Like the expanded form there is a **standard form** of every number. It is the usual numerical representation of any number.
For example 8526 is a standard form.
Expanded form: 80,000 + 2,000 + 600 + 50 + 6
Standard form : 82,656

2. Change the given expanded form to the standard form.

   a.   70,000 + 6,000 + 200 + 70 + 9

   ....

   b.   90,000 + 5,000 + 800 + 80 + 7

   ....

   c.   30,000 + 8,000 + 700 + 60 + 1

   ....

   d.   40,000 + 2,000 + 500 + 30 + 8

   ....

Enjoy with Numbers

1. Fill in the boxes with > or < (smaller than/bigger than)
   a. 6280 ☐ 8026
   b. 62589 ☐ 62489

2. Fill in the missing numbers.
   a. 360, 1360, ☐, 3360
   b. 65331, 64331, 63331, ☐, 61331

3. a. Round off 394 to the nearest tens = ☐
   b. Round off 185 to the nearest hundred = ☐

4. Write in words:-
   a. 7,43,815 = _____
   b. 65,058 = _____

5. Write the following in numerals:-
   a. Eight thousand eighty hundred and twelve = ☐
   b. Two lakhs forty six thousand three hundred and thirty = ☐

6. In the number 8,65,174
   a. The digit 1 is in the ☐ place.
      The value of the digit is ☐
   b. The digit ☐ is in thousands place.
      The value of the digit is ☐

Word Problems (Addition)

In an exhibition tourists in large numbers came to visit on the first 4 days of the week. How many tourists visited the exhibition during four days? Write the answer in words too.

Tourists who visited exhibition in four days as follows:

Monday	–	64250
Tuesday	–	70588
Wednesday	–	50890
Thursday	–	26588

```
    T Th  Th  H  T  0
     6    4   2  5  0  ← Monday
     7    0   5  8  8  ← Tuesday
     5    0   8  9  0  ← Wednesday
  +  2    6   5  8  8  ← Thursday
  ─────────────────────
   2, 1   2,  3  1  6
```

Answer: Two lakh twelve thousand three hundred and sixteen tourists visited exhibition during those four days

1. A business man earned profit in six months which was as follows:

    January → Rs. 80,880
    February → Rs. 68,008
    March → Rs. 26,508
    April → Rs. 45,800
    May → Rs. 60,000
    June → Rs. 8,900

    How much total money did the business man get as profit during those six months? Write the amount of money in words too.

Month		T Th	Th	H	T	O
January	→	8	0	8	8	0
February	→					
March	→					
April	→					
May	→					
June	→					
Total Profit	→					

Profit in rupees

Answer: The businessman got total Rs. _____ as profit during those six months. (_____ lakh _____ thousand_____ hundred and _____)

2. A book seller sold 35,900 books on the first day, 28,654 on the second day and 2,869 books on the third day and 973 books on the fourth day. How many books did he sell in those four days?

		T Th	Th	H	T	O
First day	→	•	•	•	•	•
Second day	→	•	•	•	•	•
Third day	→		•	•	•	•
Fourth day	→	+		•	•	•
Total number of books	→					

Answer: The book seller sold _____ books in four days.

3. Add :-
   7000 + 700 + 70 + 7 = _____

4. On Christmas, Robert purchased a car for Rs. 7,50,000, a computer which costed for Rs. 75,895, a watch which costed him Rs. 15,000 and a box of chocolates worth Rs. 500. How much money does Robert spent on Christmas day?

	L	T Th	Th	H	T	O
Cost of the car →	•	•	•	•	•	•
Cost of the computer →		•	•	•	•	•
Cost of the watch →		•	•	•	•	•
Cost of the chocolate box →	+			•	•	•
Total money spent →						

Answer: Robert spent total Rs. _____ on Christmas Day.

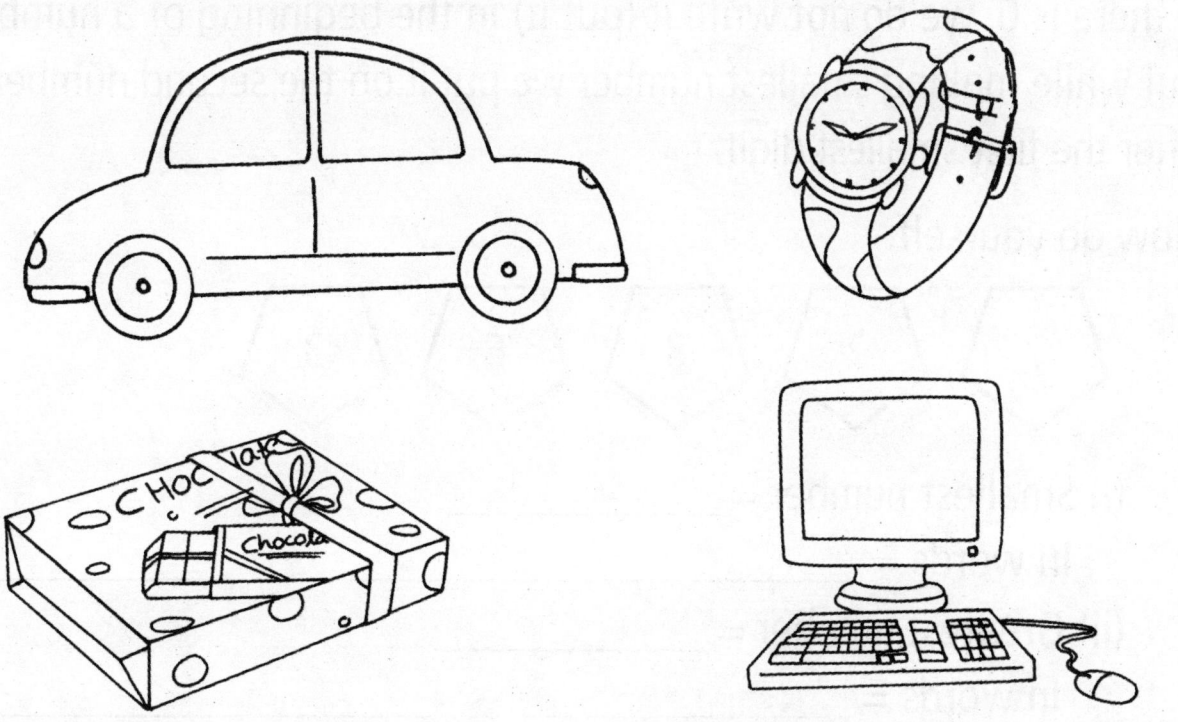

Building of Numbers

Make the smallest and the biggest numbers out of the numbers given below. Do write their name in words too. One example is done for you.

Example:- 8, 2, 9, 2, 5, 1

Write the number in the increasing order to get the smallest number and in the decreasing order to get the biggest number.

Smallest number = 1,22,589
(Increasing order)

Largest or biggest number = 9,85,221
(Decreasing order)

Answer: Smallest number will be 1,22,589

One lakh twenty two thousand five hundred and eighty nine

Biggest number will be 9,85,221

Nine lakh eighty five thousand two hundred and twenty one.

Remember

If there is 0, we do not write it (put it) in the beginning of a number but while making smallest number we put it on the second number just after the first smallest digit.

Now do yourself:-

1. 7, 2, 8, 6, 3

  (i) Smallest number = _____
    In words = _____
  (ii) Greatest number = _____
    In words = _____

2.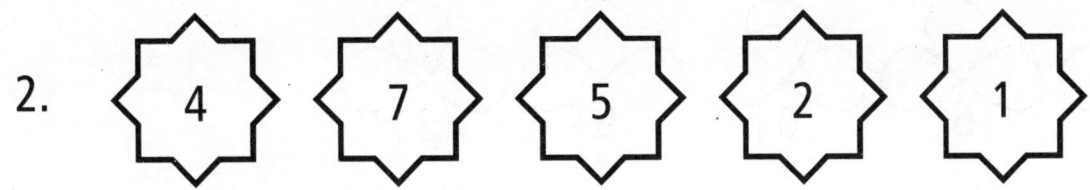

    (i) Smallest number = _____
        In words = _____

    (ii) Greatest number = _____
         In words = _____

3.

    (i) Smallest number = _____
        In words = _____

    (ii) Greatest number = _____
         In words = _____

4.

    (i) Smallest number = _____
        In words = _____

    (ii) Greatest number = _____
         In words = _____

5.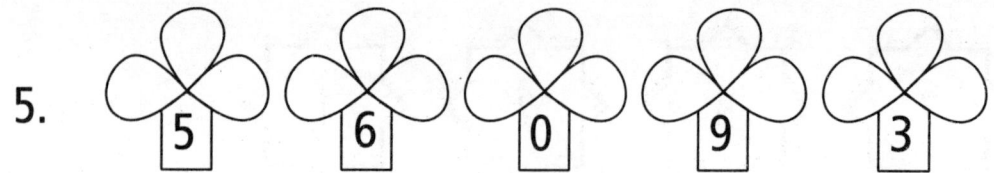

    (i) Smallest number = _____
       In words = _____

    (ii) Greatest number = _____
       In words = _____

6.

    (i) Smallest number = _____
       In words = _____

    (ii) Greatest number = _____
       In words = _____

7. ◇2◇ ◇9◇ ◇7◇ ◇3◇ ◇1◇

    (i) Smallest number = _____
       In words = _____

    (ii) Greatest number = _____
       In words = _____

Word Problems (Subtraction)

1. There are 19,828 books in a shop. The book seller sold 9,828 books in one week. How many books remained in the shop?

	T Th	Th	H	T	O
Total number of books →	•	•	•	•	•
Number of books sold →	−	•	•	•	•
Books remained in the shop →					

Answer: Total number of books which remained in the shop ☐

2. If you have Rs. 2,000 and you wish to buy a watch worth Rs. 2,500. How much more money would you need to pay to purchase the watch?

	Th	H	T	O
Money you require →	•	•	•	•
Money you have →	−	•	•	•	•
Money you need more →				

Answer: I would require Rs. ☐ more to purchase a watch worth Rs. 2500.

3. A manager gets Rs. 80,000 salary per month from an office. He saved Rs. 15,000 each month. How much did he spend in a month?

   Money earned → Rs. 8 0 0 0 0
   Money saved → Rs. 1 5 0 0 0

   Money spent = Rs. 80,000 – Rs. 15,000

Answer : Rs. ☐

4. If there are 28,84,278 men and 28,78,463 women in a city. How many men were more than women?

   Total number of men   →   2 8 8 4 2 7 8
   Total number of women → – 2 8 7 8 4 6 3
   Difference of
   men and women   _____

Answer: ☐ men are more than women in the city.

5. There were 87,808 students who appeared for X board exam. 80,929 students passed the examination. How many students failed in the X board exam?

   Total number of students   →   8 7 8 0 8
   Number of Students who
   passed X Board   → –   8 0 9 2 9
   Number of Students failed in   →   _____
   the X examination

Answer: ☐ students failed in the X board examination.

Prime and Composite Numbers

Remember

One is a factor of all the numbers.

☞ 1 × 1 = 1

One has only one factor so it is neither a prime number nor a composite number.

☞ 2 × 1 = 2

Two is the only prime number which is even. All other prime numbers are odd.

Number 2 have only two factors one and the number itself.

☞ Numbers which have factors other than 1 and themselves are called Composites Numbers.

A number list of Prime and Composite numbers from 1-12

Number		Factors
①	Neither a prime number, nor a composite number.	①
②	Prime number	①, ②
③	Prime number	①, ③
④	Composite number	①, ②, ④
⑤	Prime number	①, ⑤
⑥	Composite number	①, ②, ③, ⑥
⑦	Prime number	①, ⑦
⑧	Composite number	①, ②, ④, ⑧
⑨	Composite number	①, ③, ⑨
⑩	Composite number	①, ②, ⑤, ⑩
⑪	Prime number	①, ⑪
⑫	Composite number	①, ②, ③, ④, ⑥, ⑫

Fractions

When we divide a whole object into parts or when we break something into parts, it is called a fraction.

See and understand:–

$1 = \left(\frac{1}{4} + \frac{1}{4} + \frac{1}{4} + \frac{1}{4}\right)$ $\frac{1}{2} = \left(\frac{1}{4} + \frac{1}{4}\right)$ $\frac{1}{4} = \frac{1}{4}$ $\frac{1}{4} + \left(\frac{1}{4} + \frac{1}{4} + \frac{1}{4}\right)$

a. $\frac{1}{4} + \frac{1}{4}$ = $\frac{1}{4} + \frac{1}{4} = \left(\frac{1}{2}\right)$

b. $\frac{1}{4} + \frac{1}{4} + \frac{1}{4}$ = $\frac{1}{4} + \frac{1}{4} + \frac{1}{4} = \left(\frac{3}{4}\right)$ or $\frac{1}{4} + \frac{1}{2} = \left(\frac{3}{4}\right)$

c. $\frac{1}{4} + \frac{1}{4} + \frac{1}{4} + \frac{1}{4}$ = $\frac{1}{4} + \frac{1}{4} + \frac{1}{4} + \frac{1}{4} = \left(1\right)$ or $\frac{1}{2} + \frac{1}{2} = \left(1\right)$ or $\frac{1}{4} + \frac{3}{4} = \left(1\right)$

1. Do it yourself. One has been done for you.

a. $\left(\frac{1}{2}\right) = \frac{1}{4} + \boxed{\frac{1}{4}}$ b. $\left(\frac{3}{4}\right) = \frac{1}{4} + \frac{1}{4} + \boxed{}$

c. $\left(\frac{3}{4}\right) = \frac{1}{2} + \boxed{}$ d. $\left(1\right) = \frac{1}{2} + \boxed{}$

2. Tom's mother has one apple. She divided it into two equal parts and gave to Tom. How much remained in his mother's hand?

Answer: Tom's mother had ☐ apple.

3. Robert had one cake. He divided it into four parts to share it with his three sisters. All of them got an equal share and enjoyed it. How much of the cake did Robert eat?

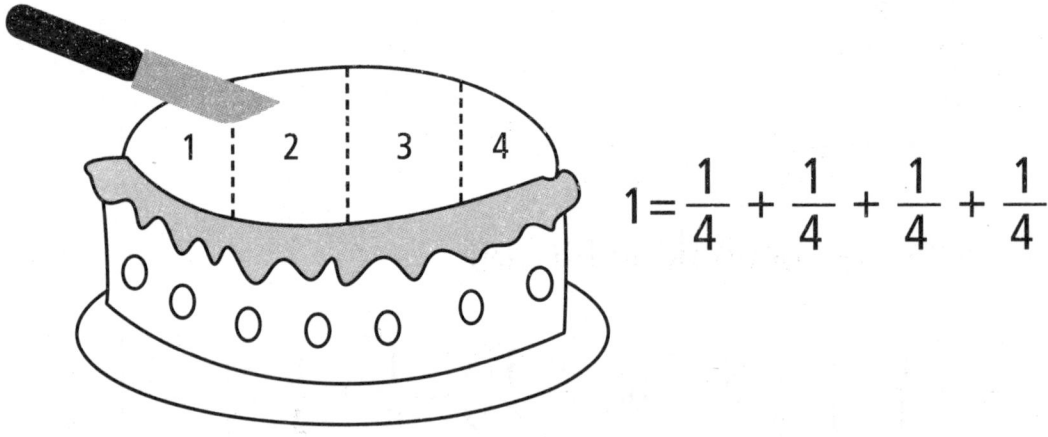

Answer: Robert ate ☐ of the cake.

4. Add and see:-

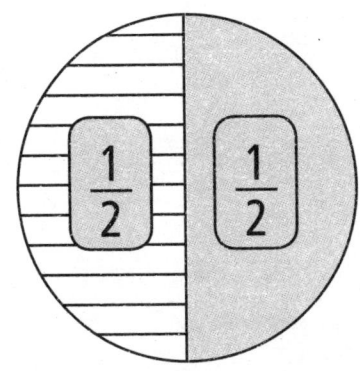

$\frac{1}{2} + \frac{1}{2} =$ ◯1   One

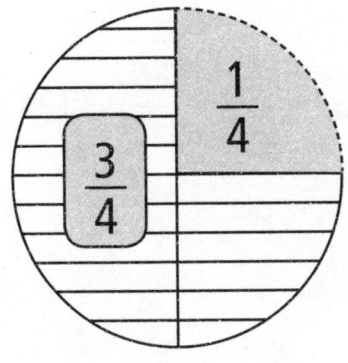

$= \frac{1}{4} + \frac{3}{4} = \square$

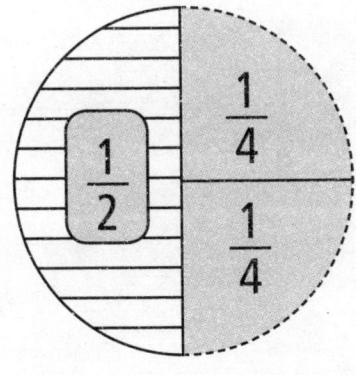

$\frac{1}{2} + \frac{1}{4} + \frac{1}{4} = \square$

$\frac{1}{4} + \frac{1}{4} + \frac{1}{4} + \frac{1}{4} = \square$

5. See the shaded portions and fill in the boxes.

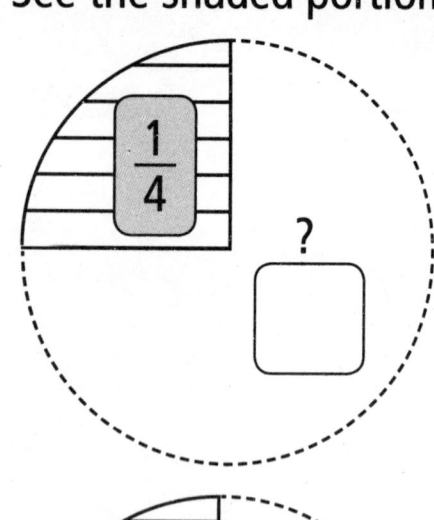

$\dfrac{1}{4} = \bigcirc$?

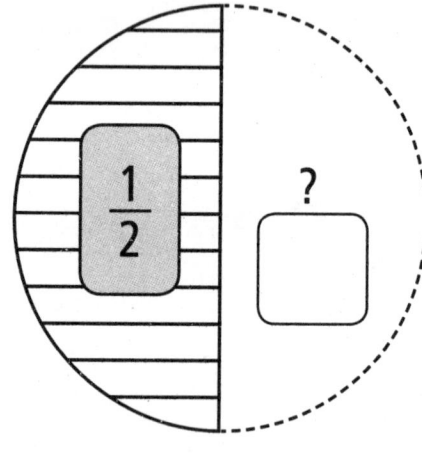

$\dfrac{1}{2} = \dfrac{1}{4} + \dfrac{1}{4}$

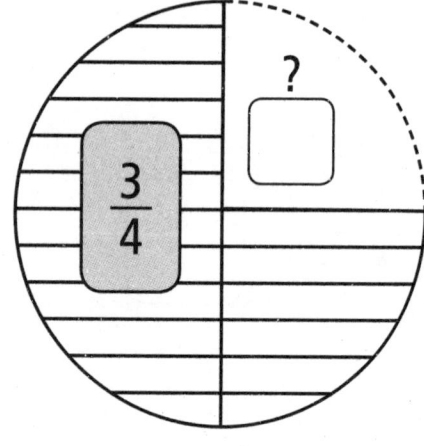

$\dfrac{3}{4} = \dfrac{1}{2} + \dfrac{1}{4}$

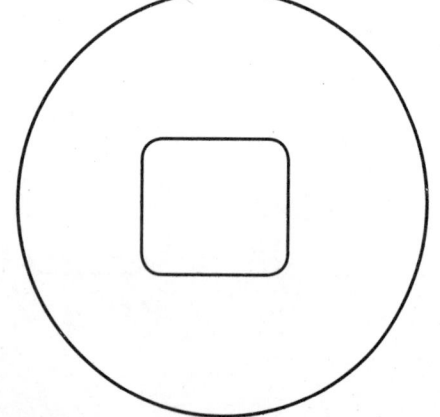

=

6. Break up the fractions into numerator and denominator

   Numerator   denominator

   a. $\dfrac{2}{3}$ =   3

   b. $\dfrac{8}{9}$ =   ☐

   c. $\dfrac{8}{9}$ =   ☐

7. Write the fraction for the shaded portion.

   a. 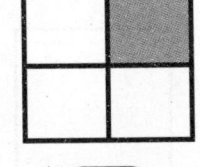 ☐

   b. 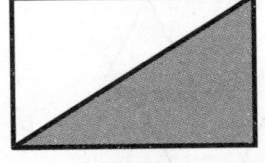 ☐

   c.  ☐

   d. 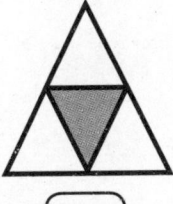 ☐

   e. 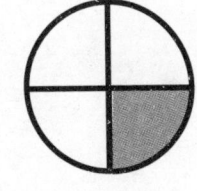 ☐

   f. 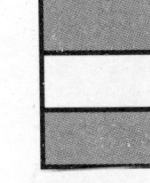 ☐

   g.  ☐

   h.  ☐

   i. 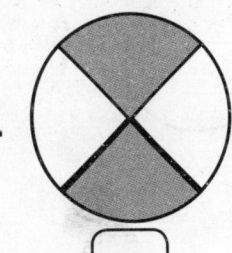 ☐

   j. 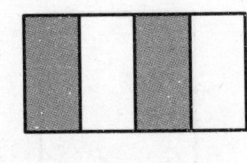 ☐

   k. 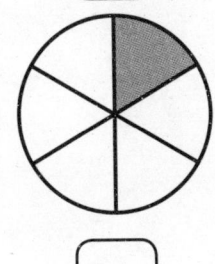 ☐

   l. 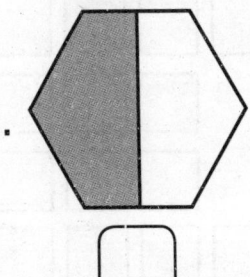 ☐

8. What part of each group is shaded?

a.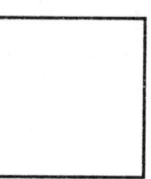

b.

c.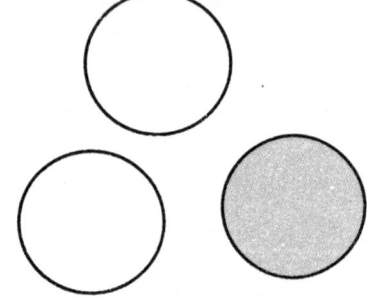

d.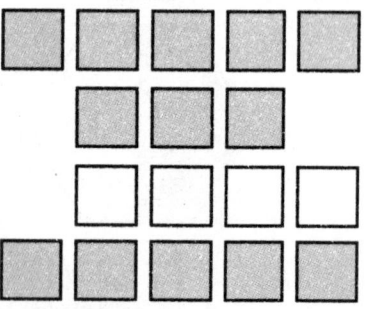

Symbols

Put the correct symbols in the box. Remember, value of the numbers on both the sides should be equal. A few have been done for you.

1. 18 ÷ 2 = 9 × 1 = 9

2. 50 − 10 = 10 × 4 = 40

3. 6 × 6 = 30 + 6 = 6

4. 12 ☐ 3 = 44 ☐ 40 =

5. 10 ☐ 2 = 4 ☐ 2 =

6. 10 ☐ 2 = 22 ☐ 10 =

7. 16 ☐ 8 = 23 ☐ 21 =

8. 9 ☐ 8 = 20 ☐ 3 =

9. 25 ☐ 5 = 30 ☐ 25 =

10. 100 ☐ 2 = 60 ☐ 10 =

Division
Remember
In Division:-
- The number to be divided is called the **dividend**.
- The number with which we divide is called **divisor**.
- The answer we get after division is called **quotient**.
- The number we are left with in the end is called the **remainder**.

Example:- 1

$$\begin{array}{r} 5 \\ 4\overline{)21} \\ -20 \\ \hline 1 \end{array}$$

Divisor ← 4, Dividend = 21, Quotient = 5, Remainder = 1

Dividend = (Divisor x Quotient) + Remainder

21 = (4 x 5) + 1
21 = 20 + 1
21 = 21

Here, Dividend = 21
Divisor = 4
Quotient = 5
Remainder = 1

Example:- 2

$$\begin{array}{r} 16 \\ 4\overline{)66} \\ -4 \\ \hline 26 \\ -24 \\ \hline 2 \end{array}$$

Here, Dividend = 66
Divisor = 4
Quotient = 16
Remainder = 2

Properties of division:-

- If the dividend is zero and the divisor is a non-zero number, the quotient is = 0

  Example:- $0 \div 8 = 0$
  $0 \div 15 = 0$

- If the divisor is 1, the quotient will be equal to the divident.

  Example:- $19 \div 1 = 19$
  $73 \div 1 = 73$

- If the dividend and the divisor are the same non-zero number, the quotient is 1.

  Example:- $6 \div 6 = 1$
  $60 \div 60 = 1$
  $431 \div 431 = 1$

Note:-
- Dividend ÷ Divisor = Quotient
  $56 \div 7 = 8$
- Divisor × Quotient = Dividend
  $7 \times 8 = 56$

1. Do your self:-

    a. 64 ÷ 8 = _____
    b. 33 ÷ 3 = _____
    c. 66 ÷ 11 = _____
    d. 100 ÷ 10 = _____
    e. 120 ÷ 12 = _____

2. Find the quotient and the remainder without actual division.

			Quotient	Remainder
a.	87 ÷ 10		_____	_____
b.	484 ÷ 100		_____	_____
c.	250 ÷ 10		_____	_____
d.	2080 ÷ 100		_____	_____
e.	1857 ÷ 1000		_____	_____

3. Divide and write the Dividend, Divisor, Quotient and Remainder.

		Dividend	Divisor	Quotient	Remainder
Example:-	45 ÷ 5 = 9	45	5	9	0
a.	83 ÷ 9 = ____	83	9	9	0
b.	100 ÷ 10 = ____	____	____	____	____
c.	60 ÷ 5 = ____	____	____	____	____
d.	151 ÷ 10 = ____	____	____	____	____
e.	112 ÷ 11 = ____	____	____	____	____
f.	408 ÷ 100 = ____	____	____	____	____
g.	580 ÷ 500 = ____	____	____	____	____
h.	1000 ÷ 100 = ____	____	____	____	____
i.	360 ÷ 300 = ____	____	____	____	____
j.	400 ÷ 40 = ____	____	____	____	____

Remember: Dividend ÷ Divisor = Quotient

Example:- 45 ÷ 5 = 9

Divisor x Quotient = Dividend

5 x 9 = 45

4. Solve:-

a. 7)245   Answer : _____

b. 8)656   Answer : _____

c. 10)110   Answer : _____

Word Problems (Division)

1. If you have to divide 30 mangoes equally among 10 children, how many mangoes will each child get?

   30 mangoes ÷ 10 mangoes = ☐ mangoes each child will get.

2. If you have to divide Rs. 100 equally among ten 10 boys. How much money will each boy get?

   Rs. 100 ÷ Rs. 10 = Rs. ☐ each boy will get

3. If you have two dozen bananas and you give 2 bananas to each boy. How many boys will get the bananas?

   $\dfrac{2 \times 12}{2}$ = 24 ÷ 2 = ☐ boys will get 2 bananas each.

4. If the cost of five 5 pencils is Rs. 25. What will be the cost of one pencil?

   25 ÷ 5 = Rs. ☐

   Cost of one pencil will be = ☐

5. If the cost of 10 apples is Rs. 100, how will you calculate the cost of one apple? What is the cost of one apple ? Tick the correct answer.

   Will you | add | | substract | | multiply | or | divide | 100 and 10 to know the cost of one apple.

6. You had 36 toffees and you divided these toffees equally among your 9 friends on your birthday. How many sweets did each friend will get?

   ....
   ....
   ....

7. Robert took 24 juice cans from a shop and distributed it equally among 8 children. How many juice cans did each child received?

   ....
   ....
   ....

8. Tom purchased 100 sweets for his friends. He gave 20 sweets to each. How many friends did he have?

   ....
   ....
   ....

Multiples

Example:-

☞ • • • • •   5 x 1 = 5

☞ • • • • •
  • • • • •   5 x 2 = 10

☞ • • • • •
  • • • • •   5 x 3 = 15
  • • • • •

☞ • • • • •
  • • • • •
  • • • • •   5 x 4 = 20
  • • • • •

☞ • • • • •
  • • • • •
  • • • • •   5 x 5 = 25
  • • • • •
  • • • • •

Note:- Here 5, 10, 15, 20, 25.... are multiples of 5 which we get on multiplying 5 by 1, 2, 3, 4, 5, ...

So, we can get multiples of any number.

Multiple of 2 are 2, 4, 6, 8, 10, 12, 14, 16, 18, 20, 22, 24

1. Think and write:-

   a. First five multiples of 6 are   6, 12, 18, ___, ___.
   b. First five multiples of 9 are   9, 18, ___, ___, ___.
   c. First five multiples of 10 are   10, ___, ___, ___, ___.
   d. First five multiples of 12 are   12, 24, ___, ___, ___.

Remember

2 is a multiple of 2

4 is a multiple of 4.

So, a number is a multiple itself and every number is a multiple of 1.

Factors

Remember

    1 is a factor of every number

    Every number is a factor of itself.

Example:- 1

    63 is a multiple of 7 and 9 because $7 \times 9 = 63$

    40 is a multiple of 5 and 8 because $5 \times 8 = 40$

    $8 \times 5 = 40$

So, 7 and 9 are factors of 63

    5 and 8 are factors of 40

    6 and 10 are factors of 60 ($6 \times 10 = 60$)

    3, 4 and 5 are factors of 60 ($3 \times 4 \times 5 = 60$)

    So each number is a factor of the product.

Remember

A number should be exactly divided by its all factors so that in division sums, the remainder is zero (0).

Example:- 2

    3 and 4 are factors of 12 ($3 \times 4 = 12$)

    but 12 has other factors also

$$1\overline{)12} = 12 \quad 2\overline{)12} = 6 \quad 6\overline{)12} = 2 \quad 12\overline{)12} = 1$$

(remainder × in each case)

The quotient obtained is also a factor of the number divided.

Example:- 3
Find all the factors of 80.

```
    80        40        20        16        10
 1)  80    2)  80    4)  80    5)  80    8)  80
    -80       -80       -80       -80       -80
     x         x         x         x         x

     6         5         4         2         1
 2) 12    16)  80    20) 80    40) 80    80) 80
    -12       -80       -80       -80       -80
     x         x         x         x         x
```

So, these are the multiplication factors of 80

80 has 5 pairs of ⟶
factors

I. $1 \times 80 = 80 = (1 \text{ and } 80) = 80 \times 1 = 80$

II. $2 \times 40 = 80 = (2 \text{ and } 40) = 40 \times 2 = 80$

III. $4 \times 20 = 80 = (4 \text{ and } 20) = 20 \times 4 = 80$

IV. $5 \times 16 = 80 = (5 \text{ and } 16) = 16 \times 5 = 80$

V. $8 \times 10 = 80 = (8 \text{ and } 10) = 10 \times 8 = 80$

So, all the factors of 80 are 1, 2, 4, 5, 8, 10, 16, 20, 40, 80

Example:-

Find all the factors of 50.

50 has 3 pairs of factors

(1 and 50), (2 and 25), (5 and 10)

1 x 50 = 50   50 x 1 = 50
5 x 10 = 50   10 x 5 = 50
2 x 25 = 50   25 x 2 = 50

Answer: All the factors of 50 are 1, 2, 5, 10, 25 and 50

Complete the list (Fill the blocks)

Numbers	Factors
1	1 (Number one has only one factor 1 is considered neither a prime nor a composite number.)
2	1, 2 (only two factors, 1 and the number itself)
3	1, 3 (only two factors, 1 and the number itself)
4	1, 2, 4
5	1, 5 (only two factors 1 and the number itself)
6	1, 2, 3, 6
7	1, 7 (only two factors 1 and the number itself)
8	1, ☐, ☐, 8
9	1, ☐, ☐
10	1, ☐, 5, ☐

Measurement
Metre and Centimetre

- Take an inch-tape and a piece of chalk. Put a mark in front of your toes from where you start walking. Walk slowly. Now start counting your ten steps in one direction. Put a mark using chalk near your toes. Measure the distance with an inch-tape. Write how much distance you covered in your ten steps = ☐ metre.

- Divide the covered distance with 10. Write the distance covered in your one step = ☐

Remember
1 metre = 100 cm

1. Convert metre into centimetre:-

    1 metre = 100 cm

    5 metre = 5 x 100 = 500 cm

    8 metre = 8 x 100 = ☐

    2.5 metre = 2 x 100 + 50 ☐

2. Convert kilometre into metre:-
    a. 1 km = 1000 m
    b. 7 km = 7 x 1000 = ☐
    c. 10 km = 10 x 1000 = ☐
    d. 5.5 km = 5 x 1000 + 500 = ☐

Capacity

Measuring capacity

The capacity of a vessel tells us how much it can contain.

For example:-

    One litre = 1000 millilitres

or 1 l   = 1000 ml or 1000 cube centimetres

    1 l   = 1000 cc

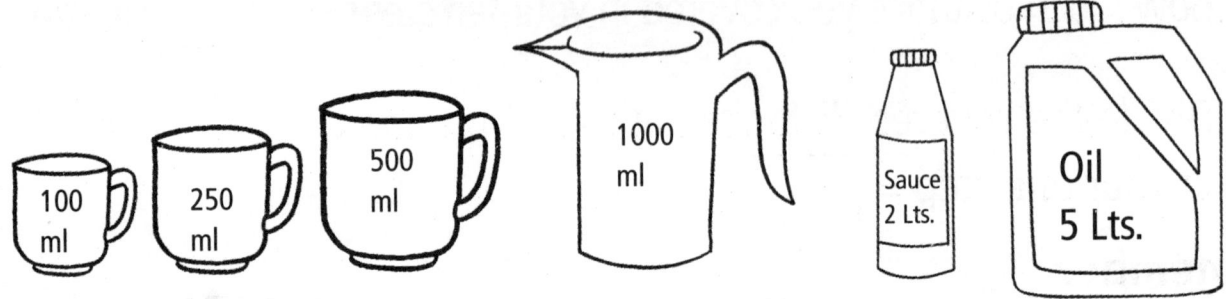

➢ How many cups/mugs you can fill if you have only one litre milk and the capacity of mugs are 500 ml?

Answer: 2 cups of the capacity of 500 ml each.

    500 + 500 = 1000 ml = 1 Litre

or 500 x 2 = 1000 ml = 1l

Answer: We can fill only 2 mugs in one litre.

➢ If we have mugs having capacity of 250 ml each. How many cups can be filled with one litre of milk?

250 x 4 = [250 ml] + [250 ml] + [250 ml] + [250 ml] =

Answer: 4 cups

➢ If each cup has a capacity of 100 ml. How many cups can be filled in 1l milk?

100 x ? = 1000 ml.

➢ Measuring cylinders are used to measure capacity.

1   One litre = 1000 ml or 1000 cc

$\frac{1}{2}$ Half litre = 500 ml or 500 cc

$\frac{1}{4}$ Quarter litre = 250 ml or 250 cc

There is 800 ml orange juice in the measuring cylinder. If we have glasses having capacity of 200 ml, how many glasses we can fill with is 800 ml orange juice?

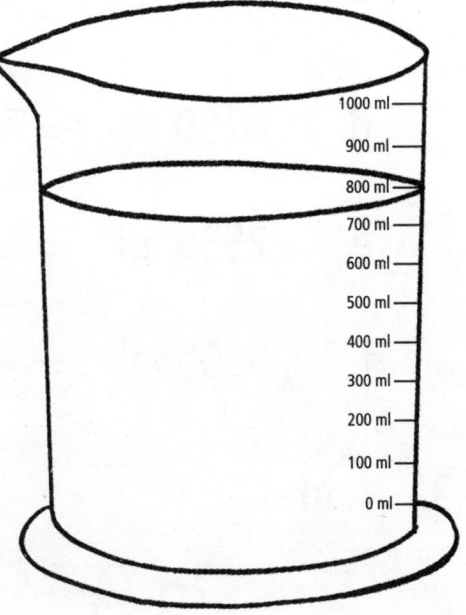

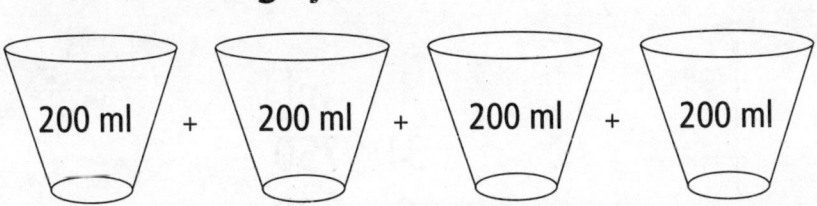

200 ml x ☐ = 800 ml   (800 ÷ 200) = 4 $\frac{\overset{4}{800}}{200}$ = 4 glasses

Answer: ☐ glasses wtih capacity 200 ml each can be filled in 800 ml orange juice

1. Fill up the blanks.
    a. One litre = 1000 ml
    b. Two litre = _____ ml
    c. Three and a quarter litres = _____ ml.
    d. One and a half litres = _____ ml.
    e. Two and a quarter litres = _____ ml.

2. Fill in the stars:-

   a. 1 l 200 ml = ☆ ml

   b. 4 l 500 ml = ☆ ml

   c. 3 l 250 ml = ☆ ml

   d. 6250 ml = ☆ l ☆ ml

   e. 2550 ml = ☆ l ☆ ml

   f. 5500 ml = ☆ l ☆ ml

3. Add:-

   ```
       l     ml
      55    250
   +  15    500
   ─────────────
   ```
   Answer: ☐ l ☐ ml

4.
   ```
       l     ml
      31    750
   +   9    200
   ─────────────
   ```
   Answer: ☐ l ☐ ml

5. Subtract:-

   ```
       l     ml
      85    750
   -  25    500
   ─────────────
   ```
   Answer: ☐ l ☐ ml

6.
   ```
        l     ml
      101    500
   -   91    250
   ─────────────
   ```
   Answer: ☐ l ☐ ml

7. You are intelligent. You can solve these simple problems. One has been done for you.

   a. I have one litre of milk. I want to share it equally among 5 boys. How much milk each boy will get?

   1 litre milk = 1000 ml ÷ 5 = 200 ml each

Answer: Each boy will get 200 ml milk.

200 + 200 + 200 + 200 + 200 = 1000 ml

   b. We buy 4 litres milk every day for daily use. How much milk we use in one week?

   4 litres x 7 days = ☐

Answer: We use = ☐ litres of milk in one week

   c. If there is 15 litres of water in one bucket and 20 litres in another bucket what will be the total quantity of water in both the buckets?

First Bucket = ☐ l
Second Bucket = ☐ l
          + _____
            _____

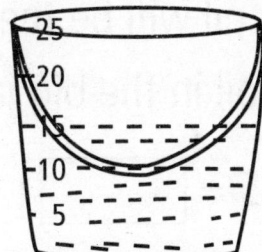
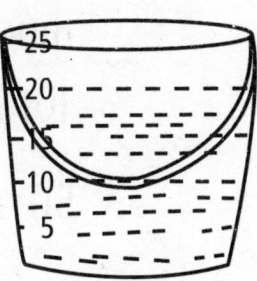

Answer: Total quantity of water is ☐ l

d. A big flask contained 5 litre of coffee. 2 litre 500 ml was used. How much coffee is left in the flask?

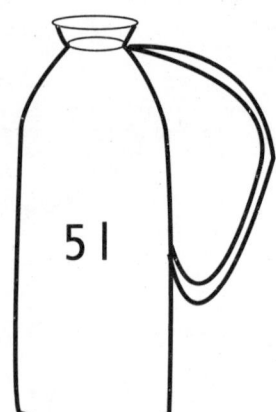

Total amount of coffee = 5 l
Coffee used = 2l 500 ml
Coffee left =   5l
         − 2l 500 ml
         ☐ Left

Answer: _____ l _____ ml coffee has left in the flask.

e. We had only 5 litre of petrol in our car. How much petrol should we buy to fill the tank having capacity of 100 litres?

100 − 5 = ☐ litre

☐ litres required.

Answer: We should buy _____ litre petrol to fill the tank.

f. There is a big jar of mustard oil having 50 litre oil. We want to distribute this oil equally into five small containers. How much oil will be there in each container?

Total oil in the big jar = 50 l

50 ÷ 5 = ☐ l

Answer: Each container will have ☐ l of mustard oil.

Roman Numerals

There are seven basic symbols to represent Roman numerals.

Roman Numerals	I	V	X	L	C	D	M
Hindu-Arabic Numerals	1	5	10	50	100	500	1000

Remember

Letters I, X and M can be repeated upto a maximum of three times.

III = 3

XXX = 30

mm = 2000

Letters V, L, D cannot be repeated

1. Which number is bigger?

   X   >   V

   L   ☐   XII

   V   ☐   L

   C   ☐   D

   D   ☐   C

2. Write the numbers which are equivalent to the Roman numerals.

   XX   =   20

   XIII   =   ☐

   IV   =   ☐

   VII   =   ☐

Activity Time

Materials required:-
- Match sticks or tooth picks
- Fevicol, a brush
- A white drawing sheet

Procedure:
1. Make the following pattern of squares using match sticks or tooth picks

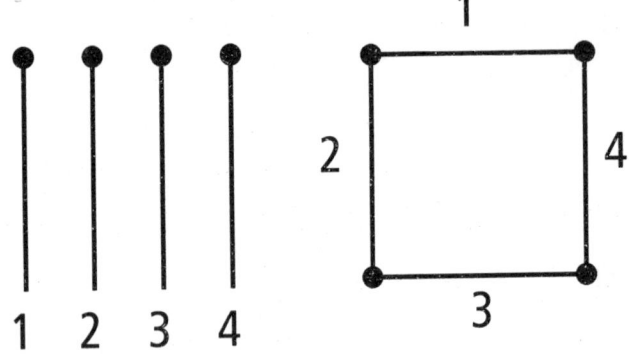

2. Make the following pattern of triangles using matchsticks or toothpicks on the white sheet of paper.

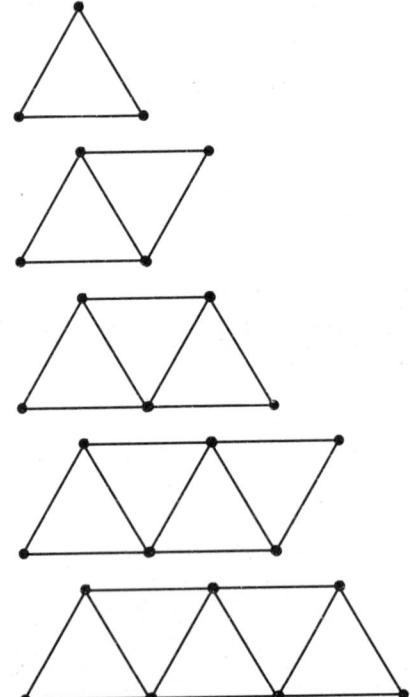

3. Make this pattern of squares given below
   How many squares are here in this picture = ☐
   How many match sticks are required to make all the squares? ☐

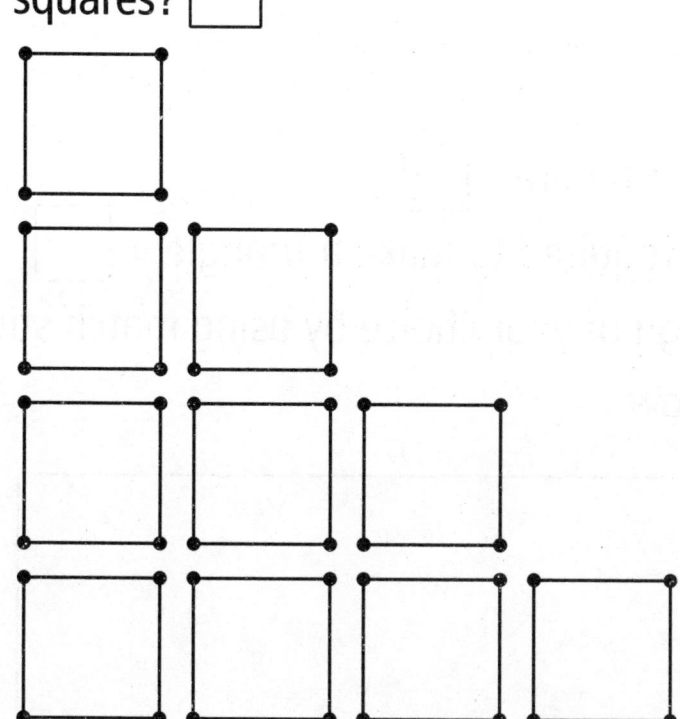

4. Now draw boxes of the number that is mentioned. Now count the number of matchsticks that will be required to make the boxes and write the number in the star.

   a. 5 ☐☐☐☐☐ ⟶ ☆

   b. 8 ———?——→ ☆

   c. 10 ———?——→ ☆

   d. 13 ———?——→ ☆

   e. 22 ———?——→ ☆

5. Observe and reply.

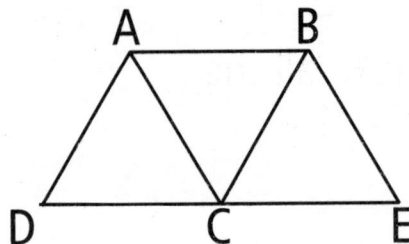

a. How many triangles are here? ☐
b. How many lines are required to make a Triangle = ☐
c. Make a pattern design of your choice by using match sticks in the box given below.

6. Draw a square of AD 5 cm in your notebook.

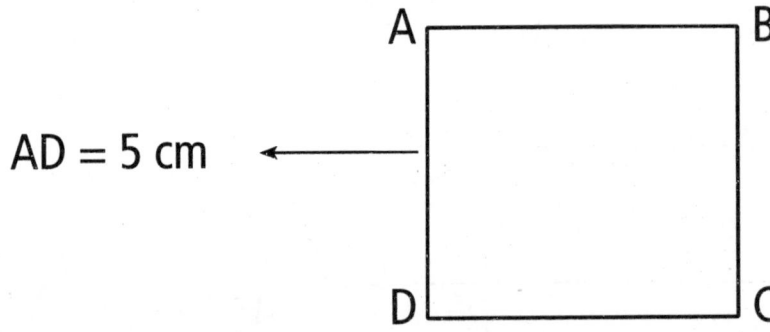

AD = 5 cm

Area

The measurement of total surface of a figure is called its **area.**

Area of a rectangle/square = length x breadth

If the length is 8 metre breadth is 6 metre

Area will be 8 x 4 = 32 square metre

Remember

➢ The unit of measurement of area is always in squares.

➢ If you know the area of a rectangle and the measurement of one of its sides, you can get the measurement of other side by dividing the area.

Example:- If length is 8 m and breadth is 4 metre

Length = Area ÷ breadth

= 32 ÷ 4 = 8

Breadth = Area ÷ length

= 32 ÷ 8 = 4

1. If a carpet is 8 metres long and 5 metres broad, find the area of the carpet?

    Area of the carpet = Length x breadth

    = ☐ x ☐

    = ☐ square metres

    Answer: Area of the carpet is ☐ square metres

Perimeter

Perimeter is the distance around a shape or the total length of the outer boundary of a figure.

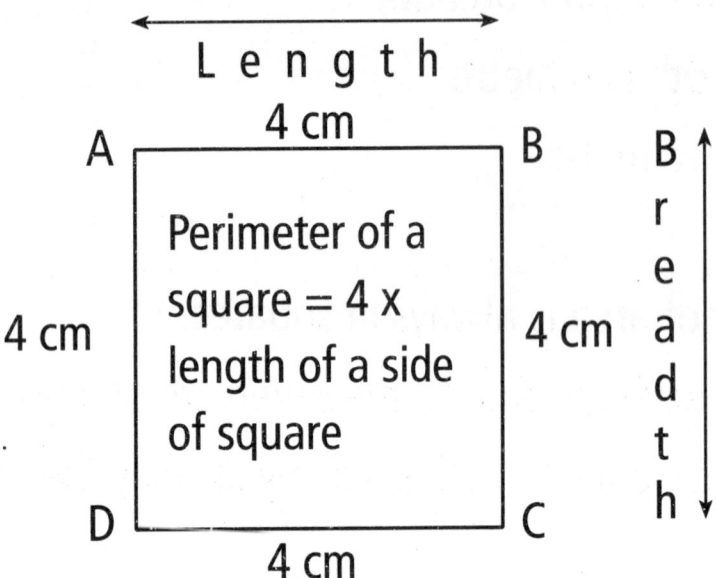

Perimeter of the above square
= 4 x 4 cm
= 16 cm

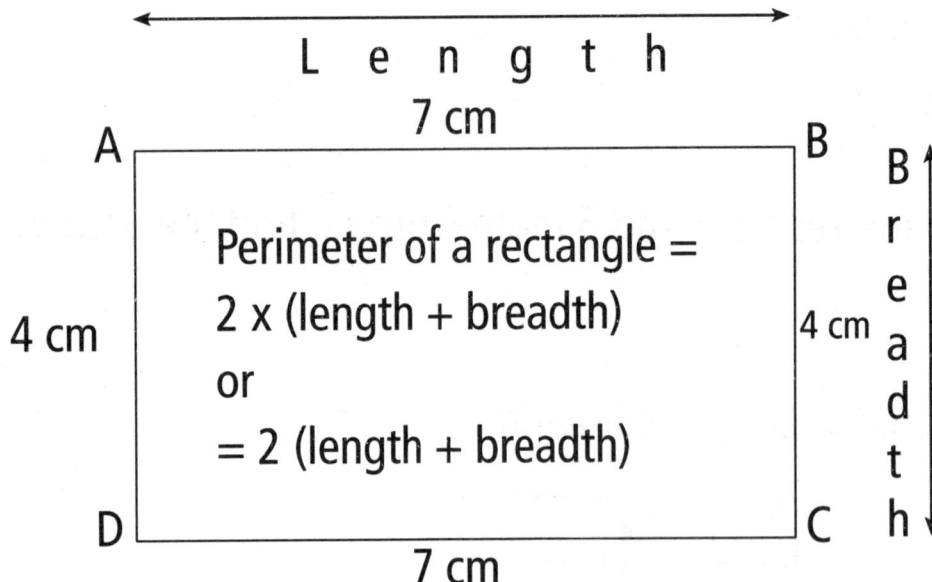

Perimeter of the above rectangle
= (2 x 7) + (2 x 4)
= 14 + 8
= 22 cm

Example:-
1. Find the perimetre of a square field whose sides are 30 metres each.
   Perimeter of the field = Number of sides x length of one side
   = 4 x 30 metre
   Perimeter = 120 metre
Answer: Perimeter of the field is 120 metres

Do yourself:-

1. Find the perimetre of a playground which is 80 metre broad and 120 metre long.
   Perimeter = 2 (length + breadth)
   = 2 (120 + 80) = ☐ metre
Answer: Playfield's perimetre is _____ metre.

2. Write the perimeter of a square of 6 cm.

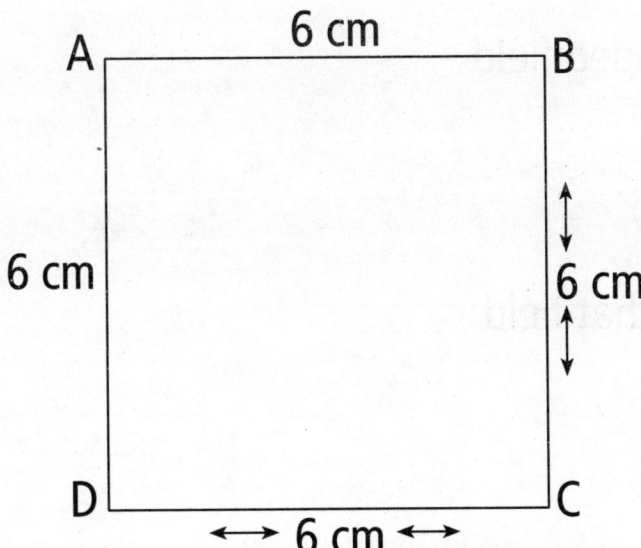

Perimeter = 2 (length + breadth)
= _____ = ☐ cm

Answer: The perimeter of the square is _____ cm

3. The length and the breadth of a swimming pool are 50 metre and 30 metre respectively. What will be its perimetre?

   Perimetre of the swimming pool

   = 2 (length + breadth)

   = 2 (50 + 30) metre

   = ☐ metre

   Answer: The perimetre of the swimming pool is ☐ metre

4. Find the perimetre of a square shaped room whose length is 15 metre.

5. A boy runs around a square field two times. Find the total distance covered by the boy if the length of the field is 250 metre. (**Remember** 1 kilometre = 1000 metres)

   Perimetre of the square shaped field

   = 4 × length of the field,

   = ☐ metre

   Boy ran two times around that field

   = 2 × perimeter

   = 2 × ☐ metre

   = ☐ kilometre.

   Answer: The boy covered total ☐ distance.